# Welcome to France – Need to know information.

### Answers to questions you didn't even know you had.

By Emma Alexander and Andrew Lockhart-Mirams

©2024

All rights reserved

**ISBN:** 9798877540361
**Imprint:** Independently published

# Forewords

Having lived and worked in France since 2002, I would like to share with you some of my experiences, including things I wish I had known before making the move. I hope you will find this guide informative and useful. It not only covers all the essential information you need to know about starting a new life in France, but also lots of information on cultural etiquette, social situations, and things to make the transition just that little bit easier. This pack differs from our other guides, (Health, Driving and Licencing, and Home), in that it is full of personal experiences and also draws on the experiences of others.

I would like to thank my great friend and co-author Andrew Lockhart-Mirams for his invaluable input, guidance, and encouragement. Without him, this book would not have been possible.

I would also like to say a massive thank you to **you,** my clients, who have reminded me of the difficulties that can be faced when trying to integrate into a new culture. I hope that you will find answers to questions you didn't even know you had!

Enjoy the read!

Emma Alexander

It has been an enormous pleasure working with Emma on this project. My French language is far short of Emma's near perfection, but I have been a consumer of the wonderful French life for over 15 years and many of the points in the book I have experienced personally, such as boundary disputes, electricity line difficulties, work contracting and privacy issues. It has, however, always been a joy to turn to Emma for her second-to-none advice on administrative problems.

Andrew Lockhart-Mirams

Table des matières

## FOREWORDS ................................................................................. 2
## INTRODUCTION .......................................................................... 8
### Water and electricity ........................................................ 12
### Internet/telephone ........................................................... 13
### Taxes ................................................................................... 14
### Import Duties ................................................................... 16
### Bank accounts ................................................................... 17
### Cheques are still in vogue!! ............................................. 18
### Other expenses to consider. ............................................ 18
## GOVERNMENT BODIES – AN OVERVIEW. .......................... 22
## THE FRENCH SYSTEMS .............................................................. 25
### Health ................................................................................. 25
### Timbres fiscales -Tax stamps ........................................... 25
### Inheritance and estate laws ............................................ 28
### Justice system .................................................................... 31
### Approved consumer protection association - Association de défense des consommateurs agréée ............................ 34
### Importing a vehicle .......................................................... 36
### Planning .............................................................................. 39
### Building works .................................................................. 39
### Contracting for work ....................................................... 40
### Running a business .......................................................... 44
### Boundaries ......................................................................... 45
### Overhanging trees ............................................................ 46
### Planting trees .................................................................... 47
### Hunting .............................................................................. 47
### Windows ............................................................................ 48
### Compliance ........................................................................ 49
### Silent times! ....................................................................... 49
### Countryside and Garden Dangers .................................. 50
### Bonfires .............................................................................. 52
## QUIRKS OF THE CULTURE ...................................................... 53
### Opening hours ................................................................... 53

HOLIDAYS AND OBSERVANCES IN FRANCE IN 2024 ................................. 54
CONCERTS AND FESTIVALS ................................................................. 56
ELECTRICITY HOURS ........................................................................... 57
OVERHEAD POWER LINES .................................................................. 57
BUYING NON-PRESCRIPTION MEDICATION ....................................... 58
NAMES AND NUMBERS ...................................................................... 59
STRIKES ............................................................................................. 61
SCHOOLS ........................................................................................... 62
WEDNESDAY AFTERNOONS AND WEEKEND SPORT ............................ 65
DIETARY REQUIREMENTS ................................................................... 66
DISABILITIES ...................................................................................... 67
MAPRIMEADAPT ............................................................................... 68
SHOPPING .......................................................................................... 69
SEASONAL SUPPLIES .......................................................................... 71
RESTAURANT IRRITATIONS ................................................................. 71
"A PARTAGER ..................................................................................... 72
SERVICE CHARGES ............................................................................. 72
WOOD TABLES AND WASPS ............................................................... 73
PET OWNING ..................................................................................... 73
EMAILS .............................................................................................. 77
KEYBOARDS ....................................................................................... 77
COLD CALLING ................................................................................... 78
PRIVACY ............................................................................................ 79
PEEING .............................................................................................. 91
GOVERNMENT DOCUMENTS .............................................................. 91

**OBSERVING THE CULTURE DIFFERENCES ............................... 92**

FORMALITIES – HANDSHAKES, BISES, AND HUGS .................................. 92
GREETINGS AND 'GOOD BYES' ............................................................ 93
EXPRESSIONS ..................................................................................... 95
"THANK YOU" .................................................................................... 96
EATING TIMES AND APEROS .............................................................. 97
KNIVES AND FOLKS! .......................................................................... 98
MUSIC IN PUBLIC PLACES. ................................................................. 99
INTEGRATING INTO LOCAL COMMUNITY. ........................................... 99
TIPPING ........................................................................................... 100

**RECENT DEVELOPMENTS ............................................................ 101**

- SOMEWHERE TO EXPRESS YOUR CUSTOMER EXPERIENCE .................. 101
- NO MORE RECEIPTS IN SHOPS ........................................................... 103

## ECOLOGY ........................................................................................ 106
- LAUNCH OF "MY ELECTRIC LEASE" IN 2024 ..................................... 106
- COMPULSORY SORTING OF BIO-WASTE .............................................. 106
- REPAIR BONUS .................................................................................. 107

## ESSENTIAL DRIVING INFORMATION ........................................ 108
- TURN OFF YOUR SPEED CAMERA DETECTORS ................ 109
- POLLUTION ....................................................................................... 110
- DON'T DRINK .................................................................................... 110
- THE SPEED LIMITS ........................................................................... 111
- Recent updates for 2024 ............................................................... 111

## WHO TO CALL IN AN EMERGENCY. .......................................... 113

## FINAL WORD ................................................................................. 116

# Introduction

France is renowned for its lovely weather, iconic landmarks, beautiful architecture, and world-famous food. To enjoy your experience to the fullest, it goes without saying that the most important thing you can do before making the move is to learn as much about the language as possible. Speaking perfect French is not essential but being prepared to have a go and having a few key phrases at your disposal will make all the difference. I truly believe that speaking fluent French when it is not your native language is almost impossible. 90% of my daily life is in French, but I don't consider myself truly bilingual as I am sure that I will be perfecting the language for the rest of my life, and the sense of achievement and enrichment this brings with it is amazing.

If you can learn as much vocabulary as possible before you come, and then launch yourself into as many social situations as possible, you will be amazed how quickly you start to understand what people are saying and have the capacity to respond. The best advice I think I can give you is to be brave, embrace the lifestyle, and you will reap the rewards! Joining in with social events, visiting your local bar or volunteering for a local charity are all great ways to integrate and hear as much of the local lingo as possible.

For many of us, the whole reason for coming to France is the weather, food, and pace of life. This is something that you may want to use as a mantra, because the 'pace of life' has its downsides!! The bureaucracy in France can be heavy going, and NOTHING is an emergency here. Most of the official paperwork that will need to be tackled if you wish to live in France, can appear to be long-winded and repetitive with lots of form filling and multiple copies of documents required but stick with it and you will eventually get the progress required!

When you are thinking about making the move to France, it is imperative to have all the correct paperwork to make your move as smooth as possible. You will be required to supply multiple copies of birth certificates, marriage and divorce certificates and/or adoption certificate along with proof of address in the form of utility bills, for multiple reasons. In France, it is commonplace for the authorities to ask for an original copy of your birth certificate less than three months old. Depending on your country of origin, these certificates may only be issued at the time of birth, so don't panic if you get a request for a recent certificate. It should be enough to explain in a cover letter the issue protocol of your country. It is also commonplace to be asked for an official translation of these certificates. This must be done by a Court-appointed translator and can be costly, so my advice would be to wait until you are asked to supply this, and not just go ahead and get everything translated beforehand.

NEVER send original copies of these documents even if they are requested, but good quality copies showing all four corners of the original certificate, and if sending by post, always send by recorded delivery with signature on receipt *(Lettre recommender avec accuser de reception)*.

It is imperative for you to be able to trace officially, with your paperwork, from your maiden/birth name to your current surname going through any steps in between.

There is of course other paperwork that you will most likely need such as ID, proof of address once you are set up in your home, possibly import or customs paperwork for your belongings, proof of health cover in whichever form it takes (see below for more information), and various other documentation depending on your specific situation.

## Water and electricity

Ok, so this may seem obvious, but if you are buying or renting, you will most likely need to set up water and electricity contracts. Depending on where you live, you may have to use a specific company, or you may have the choice of who you use. This also applies for waste water. If you are buying, your estate agent may be able to assist you with these tasks or advise you of the local companies you could use. Another port of call is the local town hall or *Mairie*. Or of course, I am always available to assist with these things!

Here I think it is pertinent to mention the chicken and egg situation! It is difficult to set up these accounts without a bank account, but it is difficult to set up a bank account without a utility bill! Please see below for information about bank accounts and some possible solutions!

## Internet/telephone

The communication network in France is in the middle of a massive overhaul, and this has created quite a few issues! Orange and SFR are the main players for internet and mobile coverage, but there are also a multitude of smaller suppliers that are quickly gaining market share! Broad band is being replaced by Fiber optics. At the end of 2023 it will no longer be possible to opt for a broadband contract, and by 2030 the current ADLS/copper network will be dismantled. It is currently free of charge to convert your broadband into Fiber optics, but you will have to change your contract and with some operators this can mean a large hike in prices, so shop around.

If you live in a rural area, connection to Fiber optics can be complicated and take many months to set up, and is often subject to line failure which again, is not repaired quickly. For those that are having problems, you might want to consider a satellite option for internet. However, Fiber optics speeds are much better than satellite and are not subject to interference in bad weather.

Mobile phone contracts can be linked to a landline/internet contract, and there are huge range of contracts and prices available. It is common practice to offer an attractive price for the first 12 months and then the contract increases substantially. If you phone your operator after the 12-month period, they can often offer a more attractive deal.

It is also possible to buy a cheap pay-as-you-go SIM card from most supermarkets if you do not want to enter into a contract.

<u>A French mobile phone number will be of great help when you are looking to set up online accounts for any of the government bodies or utilities.</u>

Taxes

You can find lots of detailed information on taxes in our Home pack, but as a quick overview, here is the most important information.

In France, the tax year runs from January to December

If you are resident in France, you must complete income tax returns even if you have no income, have income from another country, or pay tax in another country. The tax returns are done in April/May for the year before. Your tax notice then arrives at the end of the summer. Except for those who are employed by a French Company, in most cases, your tax for the preceding year will be paid in four equal instalments (September, October, November and December)

If you own a property, you will be subject to Property tax - *Taxe fonciere* and if you are second homeowners you will also have to pay Living tax - *Taxe d'habitation*. These tax notices are sent out in early autumn for the whole of that year to the person who owns the property on 1st January.

**\*Warning\*** If you buy a property in France, you can expect the tax notice to arrive in the autumn of the following year i.e. Buy in 2023 and receive your first tax notice in autumn 2024. The notice is most often sent to the address on the sales act that is signed at the Notaires office at the time of purchase, which could well be your old address in another country!

Setting up an online account with the tax office is the ideal way of communicating with them, managing payment amounts and getting copies of the tax notices. This can only be done once you have been issued with a fiscal number.

Import Duties

The foreword to this book talks about things I wish I had known before coming to France 20 years ago but what none of us knew then was the coming of Brexit and all the changes it would bring. Some major changes came about in the rules relating to import duties and apart from the rules about importing UK brought items there are separate rules for items brought into the country if you are moving to live in France.

Generally, these items are free of duty if you have owned them in the UK for more than 6 months but there are complicated rules where the items were first imported into the UK from around the world. Declarations have to be made and these completed before you move. It is essential that you cover this in good time before moving and information can be obtained from the French Douanes service. However, the key advice is to use the services of a

French Customs agent or an expert in the company doing the removal.

## Bank accounts

In recent years, it has become almost impossible to open a French bank account if you are non-European and non-resident. Even once you are resident, you will need proof of address to open an account – a utility bill – which you can't do until you have a bank account. Back to our chicken and egg situation!!!

One solution for this is to open an online bank account. There are various ones to choose from and word of mouth is a great way of finding the right one for your personal situation. Once you have the utility bill and proof of residency such as a visa for non-Europeans, or proof of normal residency for Europeans, it is much easier to open an account in your local branch. You will need to book an appointment to do this and take along all your paperwork.

Cheques are still in vogue!!

Compared to many other countries, cheques are still a very common way of paying invoices and other bills here, so once your bank account is set up, I strongly advise that you order a chequebook. From time to time, it will come in very useful!

Other expenses to consider.

Aside from the things I have already mentioned, you will need to consider the other expenses that you may have to face. Insurance is a big one, whether that is for health, home, legal protection, vehicle, life, or a multitude of other contingences! Depending on your situation, it may be necessary to have health insurance from the *first euro while you are waiting to join the French health system, or you may have to make social security contributions once you are affiliated.

*Health cover from the first euro refers to term used by insurance companies to indicate that the insurance covers the FULL cost of any expenses without any 'excess' being due from the individual concerned.

The cost of living is rising rapidly, and the exchange rate is not what it once was! If you need to exchange money on a regular basis, it is worth looking into the most cost-effective way of doing this as many banks are now charging a relatively large fee for non-French transactions.

Heating fuel and wood pellets have nearly doubled in price in the last few years and are no longer cheap heating methods.

Over the last couple of years, there has been a massive surge in households installing heat pumps and this has only been boosted by the various local and government aides available. Just be sure, that if you are looking at this as an option, you assess the future running costs, including the increase in the price of electricity as they may not prove to be as economical as promised!


It generally seems to be accepted that living in France is a little cheaper than living in England, certainly London, and, taken over a period, an ordinary weekly shop in one of the big supermarkets is likely to be say 5% cheaper than in England. Certainly, wine is much better value, and you seldom get a bad bottle even at the bottom of the price range. However, there are 4 big costs that need watching. The last two are one offs so unlikely to be repeated often but the third is an ever-present cost.

White goods

Beds

Decorating paint

Wood for carpentry

In each case the cost seems about 20% higher and paint and wood can be even more so. Also, over the last 10 years or so the quality of wood available seems to have deteriorated considerably, with a lot of the supply being in laminated sections: often with a lot of knots. Not good for carpentry or cabinet making.

# Government bodies – An overview.

**Impôts** – Tax office also known as *Service des impôts des particuliers (SIP)* and each region has its local branch where you can drop in or book an appointment for assistance. *La Trésor Public* means 'public treasure', and this building is where you'll be able to sort out everything to do with your taxes.

**CPAM** - *Caisse primaire d'assurance maladie* – Government body responsible for social security charges and health care. This is where you can apply to affiliate after the first three months of residency. Also known as *sécurité sociale* or *améli*. Once you are affiliated, you can create your online space which will enable you to keep an eye on your refunds, print off a copy of your rights, and apply for a European card if you are eligible (see the health pack for more information).

ANTS

*Agence nationale des titres sécurisés* – Online government body for vehicle registration, driving license, passports and ID cards.

### *Le Préfecture*

There are 101 préfectures in France, one for each administrative department. They are responsible for carrying out the work of the Ministry of the Interior, and so they hand out administrative documents such as driving licenses, passports, and residency cards. They also control the police and fire brigade.

***La Mairie***

The town hall is the center of administration for day-to-day life. It's where you register births, deaths, and marriages. It's also the place that takes care of everything to do with school life, such as enrolment and school lunches. In most towns, these buildings are the most elegant, and you'll often find cafés and restaurants surrounding them. In rural areas, the *Mairie* is often the soul of a French village.

***La CAF - Caisse d'allocations familiales***

The CAF is the government body responsible for allocating a variety of financial assistance to families, such as childcare allowance, housing benefit or disability allowance.

# The French Systems

Health

Most aspects of the French health care system are covered in our health pack, but what is the most important thing to bear in mind when considering coming to France is that it will take up to a year for you to become affiliated to the French health care system and you MUST be covered in the meantime. Even if you have no particular health issues, accidents can, and do happen, and for people applying for a VISA, health cover from the *first euro (see above) is essential. Travel insurance won't cut the mustard!!! Once you are affiliated, you can often upgrade your insurance to top-up insurance called a *mutuelle*, as CPAM do not cover 100% of health care costs.

*Timbres fiscales* -Tax stamps

Passport, driver's license, boat license, residence card... for all these documents, you need a tax stamp that allows you to pay the tax related to the procedure.

Many administrative procedures require the user to buy a tax stamp. This allows payment of a fee related to the application made.

The documents concerned.

You must purchase a tax stamp to do the following:

Identity card in case of loss or theft (in the case of simple renewal, the procedure is free of charge).

Passport (renewal or obtaining may be free of charge in certain cases).

Driving license in case of loss or theft.

Boat license.

Appeal of a court decision.

Long-stay visa as residence permit (VLS-TS).

Residence permit.

Resident card.

Movement document for minor foreigners (DCEM).

Travel documents for refugees

Application for French nationality.

The price varies depending on the administrative document requested.

Identity card lost or stolen: 25 €.

Passport (adult): 86 €

Passport (minor): €17 (under 15 years) or €42 (between 15 and 17 years).

Card or residence permit (in general): 225 €.

Appeal against judgment: €225.

The purchase of the tax stamp is fully digital since 1st January 2019:

The purchase is done online in a secure way on a dedicated site under the jurisdiction of the tax authorities, or on the website of the *National Securities Agency (ANTS)* at the time of application for the procedure.

The purchase can also be made from a newsagent often called a tabac with the logo « *Point de vente agréé* »

**How to get the tax stamp?**

The stamp is issued only in electronic format.

It can take two forms: one 2D code or a 16-digit identifier. It can be delivered in two different formats:

Via email: a PDF document containing a 2D code is sent to you. This code will be scanned by the officials when you submit your request (remember to check in your spam if you do not receive it).

By text message: the 16-digit identifier of your stamp is addressed to you and must be attached to your request (only available for French mobiles)

Note that the electronic tax stamp has a **validity period of 12 months.**

If you don't need it, you can claim it back within 18 months after purchase, via the dedicated online section.

## Inheritance and estate laws

Inheritance is a massive subject and I have tried below to outline the major points. Every situation is different, and my advice is to seek professional advice on this subject and ensure that your affairs are in order.

When do French inheritance law and inheritance tax in France apply to your assets?

Those who become official French residents, move to retire in France, or buy French property should consider whether French inheritance and succession laws apply to their assets. In some cases, foreigners and non-residents can choose the law of their country of nationality, but there can be some restrictions on dividing French-based assets under French succession law.

French inheritance law derives from the French civil code and operates a residence-based system regarding inheritance law. This means French inheritance law applies to all French residents regardless of nationality.

Forced heirship rules protect the direct line of descent – that is, children, grandchildren, and parents. Traditionally, the intent of this was to protect the family – for example, to stop an unscrupulous outsider from coercing an elderly person to disinherit family members.

However, forced heirship rules mean that, irrespective of any will, a certain proportion of the estate must go to the deceased's children or spouse. After this, the remainder can be distributed freely according to a French will.

Children can renounce their right to a French inheritance, if done in the presence of two notaries. This cannot be revoked after the parent's death.

Under inheritance law in France, the amount set aside as the reserve is as follows:

If there is one child, they receive 50% of the estate.

With two children, they receive 66.6% of the estate between them.

With three or more children, they receive 75% of the estate between them.

If there are no children, then the spouse can claim 25% of the estate.

A couple must be married at the time of death for the spouse to legally inherit some of the estate.

## Justice system

It's unnecessary to employ a lawyer or barrister (*avocat*– also the word for avocado pear!) in a civil case heard in a *tribunal d'instance*, where you can conduct your own case (if your French is up to the task). If you use a lawyer, not surprisingly, you must pay his fee. In a *tribunal de grande instance* you must employ a lawyer. An *avocat* can act for you in almost any court of law. A legal and fiscal adviser (*conseil juridique et fiscal*) is similar to a British solicitor and can provide legal advice and assistance on commercial, civil and criminal matters, as well as on tax, social security, labour law and similar matters.

He can also represent you before certain administrative agencies and in some courts. A bailiff (*huissier*) deals with summonses, statements, writs and lawsuits, in addition to the lawful seizure of property ordered by a court. He's also employed to notify documents officially and produce certified reports (*constats*) for possible subsequent use in legal proceedings, e.g. statements from motorists after a road accident.

A public notary (*notaire*, addressed as *Maître*) is a public official authorized by the Ministry of Justice and controlled by the Chambre des Notaires. Like a *conseil juridique* he's also similar to a British solicitor, although he doesn't deal with criminal cases or offer advice concerning criminal law. Notaires have a monopoly in the areas of transferring property, testamentary and matrimonial acts, which by law must be in the form of an authentic document (*acte authentique*), verified and stamped by a notaire. In France, property conveyance is strictly governed by French law and can be performed only by a notaire. A notaire also informs and advises about questions relating to administrative, business, company, credit, family, fiscal and private law.

With regard to private law, a notaire is responsible for administering and preparing documents relating to leases, property sales and purchases, divorce, inheritance, wills, loans, setting up companies, and buying and selling businesses. This guarantees the validity and safety of contracts and deeds, and they are responsible for holding deposits on behalf of clients, collecting taxes and paying them to the relevant authorities. Notaires' fees are fixed by the government and therefore don't vary from one notaire to another. It is commonplace for house sales to be overseen by a joint notaire that works on behalf of both the buyer and seller, but there is no prejudice if each party instructs its own notaire to act on their behalf.

Never assume that the law in France is the same as in any other country, as this often isn't the case. If you need an English-speaking lawyer, you can usually obtain a list of names from your country's embassy or a local consulate in France. Certain legal advice and services may also be provided by embassies and consulates in France, including an official witness of signatures (Commissioner for Oaths). French residents have the right to a free consultation with a lawyer; ask at your local Tribunal de Grande Instance for times. Legal aid (*aide juridictionnelle*) is available to EU citizens and regular visitors to France on low incomes.

Anyone charged with a crime is presumed innocent until proven guilty, and the accused has the right to silence. All suspects are entitled to see a lawyer within three hours of their arrest, a person under judicial investigation must be notified in writing, and an examining magistrate may not remand suspects in custody in a case they are investigating. Under France's inquisitorial system of justice, suspects are questioned by an independent examining magistrate (*juge d'instruction*). Other types of judges include *juges du siège* (arbitration judges) and *juges d'instance* (presiding judges).

## Approved consumer protection association - *Association de défense des consommateurs agréée*

The role of a consumer defense association is to inform, advise and help consumers to settle everyday disputes. It can act preventively to find amicable solutions and has the legal capacity: the ability of a person (physical or legal) to have rights and obligations and to exercise them themselves (e.g. the right to enter into a contract, the right to take legal action) to represent the private or collective interests of consumers before the courts.

15 approved national consumer associations are at your service to represent and defend you.

In addition to their activities at national level (studies, research, representation on a wide range of official and private bodies, consumer information and training), the movements are present at local level through a large number of associations.

## *Que Choisir*

Que Choisir is one of the largest and most widely used consumer associations. They describe themselves as "Expert, independent and militant, UFC-Que Choisir is a not-for-profit association. Surveys, tests, legal battles, lobbying: with its network of over 150 local associations, UFC-Que Choisir is at the service of consumers to inform, advise and defend them".

**Other organisations**

A list of other associations and the areas they cover can be found at this link.

Les associations de consommateurs | Institut national de la consommation (inc-conso.fr)

## Importing a vehicle

Under EU law, a private vehicle may be temporarily imported and used on French roads for up to six months without registering it.

Any vehicles belonging to people resident in France for more than six months must be registered. For this purpose, resident is someone who is domiciled in France for more than 183 days or who is employed in France. All imported vehicles must be registered withing 1 month of becoming resident.

Vehicles not yet registered in France can only legally be driven by residents of the country if the owner is a passenger. Visiting friends and family may drive the vehicle, as long as they are not resident in France.

Registering a UK car or vehicle in France is a relatively straightforward process, although it does require a number of different documents and there are a number of potential costs to factor in.

**Before bringing the vehicle to France:**

Ensure you have all the relevant documents needed to register your UK car in France.

Change your headlights (if applicable) and check that your car speedometer has a km reading (if not, this will need to be fitted)

**On arrival in France:**

Contact your local customs office to obtain your 846 A certificate.

Book your car in for Control Technique (if required)

Apply for your French registration paperwork known as the *Carte Grise*

When you have received your Carte Grise, request your French number plates.

Documents you will need to register the vehicle.

Your passport and valid driver's license

Proof of your French address, e.g. a utility bill less than 6 months old

Green Card insurance or proof of car insurance

Vehicle registration document or V5C (or export certificate if the registration document has been retained by the original issuing authority). You must complete the 'permanent export' section of the certificate.

Dated and signed Application for Registration of the Vehicle in: *Demande de certificat d'immatriculation (Cerfa 13750\*05)*

Car Bill of Sale

Signed *'Mandat d'immatriculation* (Cerfa 13757\*03)' form.

Certificate of Conformity

Import tax Certificate or 846 A

*Control Technique* certificate (French 'MOT') no older than 6 months (if applicable)

*Quitus fiscal* from the French tax authorities.

For more information about registration, necessary documents and driving in France, please refer to the Driving and Licensing pack.

Planning

The concept of a green belt does not seem to exist in the way you might know it! And it seems to be the case that if you can persuade your local *Mairie* to give permission you can build almost anywhere.

Also, if your neighbours apply for planning permission there is no obligation on the Mairie to tell you that there is an application or to give you a right to object. They may also be loath to give you any information about who has permission for what and who owns what. Applications for planning permission can be found on the Mairie's notice board, but you have to remember to look, otherwise you may not know!

Building works

It is almost impossible to get small building jobs done. The English contractors who have moved to France may be more willing to do these but regardless of where they come from, they are almost always "Too busy" – particularly in the Summer when all the foreigners want their holiday homes opened up. You need to make sure that anyone doing any work on your home has the correct qualifications, registration, and insurance. More information on this can be found in our Home pack.

## Contracting for work

In every case you need to be clear, and to specify, exactly what you want doing and a registered worker should provide a written quote -*devis* before the work is started. The quote may take the form of an estimate and you need to understand exactly what the proposal is. If certain costs are only estimated this should be made clear on the devis. When the work is completed, you will get a bill - *facture*. This should be receipted when paid. All the papers should give the contractor's registration and insurance details. Before starting do not be afraid to ask for a copy of the insurance policy and check that it is in date for the work proposed. The contractor's papers should also include their registration number -*siret*.

If you are moving from the UK you will certainly find that contracting for work in France proceeds in a very different way. In the UK you may get a quote and it is perfectly feasible to call the proposed contractor and discuss the pricing - particularly if you can see cheaper prices for some of the items – for example, an air-conditioning unit. In France what you see of the devis is what you get, and the contractor expects to keep, without reduction, the "mark-up" he may get when he buys in the goods from the manufacturer or wholesaler. This is the established way of working and if you challenge the pricing the contractor may walk away. This alone is a very good reason to get three quotes for any substantial piece of work.

You will also find that a substantial deposit will be asked for any major job where expensive equipment is being used. This can be a bit frightening as you pay the contractor and if he goes bust your money may be at risk and you do not own the title to the goods. In many cases this is a risk you may have to take and if a job has, say, three parts, it is best to contract for one then another and then the last one – rather than all three at once, with three times the risk. The standard deposit is around 30% and I would strongly advise against paying any more than this up front. A written schedule of payments for work completed is the ideal way of setting out both terms and conditions for both parties. The devis should also contain an estimated start date.

**Small works**

These are the ones where it is tempting to use cash and please see the notes below. Getting a proven contractor to do a small job where he/she has done work for you in the past is one thing but just accepting a contractor "off the street" can be very dangerous.It is possible to find independent artisans that are set up exactly for this type of work. Often referred to as *petit bricolage* or *homme tout faire*  They are often registered as a micro-entreprise and may even ask you to pay for the material necessary independently.

**Incomplete work**

One big problem in France can be resolving issues when the agreed work is incomplete or needs rectification. You may well, for example, hold back say the last 400 euro on a 2,000 euro contract but the contractor may have little interest in finishing the work, apparently prepared to forgo the balance payment rather than turning up to make the required corrections. You can write to them setting out what needs to be done. Sometimes this works but sadly there are times when nothing happens. There seems no real solution to this except perhaps holding back a big chunk of the contract monies. You must avoid the situation where the contractor simply goes to court for the balance and every defect needs to be recorded in writing with pictures to back up your story.

**Paying for work in cash**

Subject to certain conditions and different limits payments in cash can be made contractors. The limit is €15,000 for tax non-residents and €1,000 for tax residents. If payments exceed these limits, there can fines of up to 5% of the amount paid. The bigger problem however is that cash may be paid to workers working on the "black" who are not themselves paying tax and social charges. A big concern here is that the worker may very well be uninsured, and the making of the payment could void your own house insurance. Payment made on the "black" can give rise to massive fines or even prison.

Running a business

There are many skilled tradesmen who have retired in the UK but feel they would like to do a little work in France both to "keep their hand in" and make a little extra money. There are a number of formalities that have to be complied with and all have to be completed before work starts. You will be required to provide proof of your qualifications and experience before being allowed to run a regulated, skilled trade business and you must be approved by the *chambre de metiers*. I can advise on the process and paperwork necessary and assist in setting up your registered business in France.

## Boundaries

If you talk to anyone who has ever been involved with a boundary dispute, they will probably tell you that it was one of the most stressful events in their life – particularly as the dispute is not with e.g. a tradesman but with the person/family who live next door and with whom you want to be friends.

No two boundary disputes are the same so general advice cannot be given but the first starting point if you are moving into French property is to spend time with your Notaire making totally sure that the boundaries are absolutely clear and recognised. Being told that the boundary is "Where the hedge is" seems fine at the time but leads to certain disaster if you want to take out the hedge and put up a fence. If there is an outstanding issue about a boundary there is an obligation on your vendor to make it clear. You may need to appoint a *Geometre* – a specialist in measuring land boundaries and parcels of land to determine where the boundary is but if you do make sure that he/she is instructed on a joint basis with your neighbour so you are both bound by the result.

Overhanging trees

The general rule in England is that if a neighbour's tree overhangs your garden, you can cut the overhang off at the boundary line and then throw the cut piece back on to the neighbour's property. This is not the case in France and the owner of the tree has a legal duty to prune back the overhanging portion of the tree. Under the French Civil Code, it is the responsibility of the tree owner to maintain the tree and to prune back overhanging branches and foliage. Roots, brambles and twigs that encroach come into a different category and can be cut back. If there is an overhang, you will have to ask your neighbour to deal with it. If he/she does not do so you have the making of a neighbour dispute and, in the first place, you will need the help of your local Marie or a *conciliateur de justice* to try and mediate a resolution. If all else fails, you will have to take court proceedings.

Planting trees

You also need to be careful about planting trees close to a boundary and new trees that will be more than two meters high must not be planted within 2 meters of a boundary.

Hunting

In theory a hunter, or more usually a number of hunters, armed with rifles and accompanied by dogs trained to fetch out prey – more often than not wild boar who can rampage through crops and cause devastation – had no right to go on private land without the owner's permission. However, in 1964 the law was changed to permit this. Associations (ACCA) in all most all Departments are responsible for the proper management of hunting, but other areas have local arrangements. If any questions arise you will need to check locally. In all cases hunting is excluded withing 150-meter radius of a dwelling. Shots can be fired within the radius, but hunting cannot take place. This rule does not apply in non ACCA areas. It is possible to have your land excluded from an ACCA area, but the process is complicated. Anyone buying land over which hunting might take place would be well advised in the first place to consult the local Marie for relevant local information and rules.

Windows

Although there are sash windows in France, almost all windows are hinged at one side, or both, and open inwards. This makes cleaning them much easier and you can also have the shutters *"volet"* closed, or partially closed, with the windows open. The downside however is that you cannot use the sill for the storage of any objects or ornaments. Although it is only a tiny point, another downside is that if you get insects or flies inside you need to get them out, and a small vacuum cleaner could be useful, as opening the windows just lets them fly inside further.

## Compliance

No one tells you the compliance rules e.g.

Chimney regulations

Swimming pool safety

Noise restrictions

And all this needs to be investigated with reference to your property. Some are national rules but, more often than not, the rules vary from Commune to Commune. More information on this can be found in our Home assistance pack.

## Silent times!

Do-it-yourself and gardening work carried out by private individuals using tools or devices liable to cause discomfort due to their sound intensity, such as lawn mowers, chainsaws, drills, planers, power saws, are generally only authorised at the following times:

working days from 8 am to 12 noon and from 2 to 8 pm.

Saturdays from 9am to 12 noon and from 3 pm to 6 pm and

Sundays and public holidays: from 10 am to 12 noon, but each Marie may make their own rules as to what is acceptable. Farm working is exempt from "silent time" rules.

## Countryside and Garden Dangers

All the normal dangers exist in properties e.g. electricity and water, but one danger you need to watch out for are what are known as "processionary" caterpillars. They are particularly prevalent in the spring on both oak and pine trees but can be a problem at all other times of the year. The hairs or bristles can detach and sting your skin, passing on a very irritating and inflammatory toxic protein thaumetopoein. The hairs can cause sever skin and throat reactions, blisters, conjunctivitis, and asthma attacks.

They are officially recognised as a harmful species in France. They are called *"chenilles processionnaires"*. They move in long lines and make their nests in trees – the nests look like big white balls of candy floss, and they travel on the ground during their development. They can be found in tree bark. The pine tree version is brown in colour, and the oak version is greyish.

Like many dangerous species they are very pretty but if you see one, or a train, DO NOT TOUCH and keep well away as the hairs can detach and spread on the wind, or on animal or pet fur or gardening equipment. There have been many cases of dogs especially, being curious, loosing part of the tongue or jaw from the toxins. If you suspect contact, take a shower, and rinse off the hairs as soon as possible. In case of any suspected or worsening issues, consult a doctor as soon as possible. If you have any symptoms or are in urgent distress, call 15. You may also need to consult an anti-poison centre.

## Bonfires

Generally, but as with many things, this is something best checked with the local Marie, bonfires are only permitted between November and April and in some cases, the permitted window is even shorter. When bonfires are permitted you can only burn garden waste and not household waste. Household waste either has to be placed in the collecting bins, divided between recyclable waste or ordinary waste, or taken to the local *déchetterie*. The risk of fires spreading in hot weather is considerable and in the hot summer of 2023 a single spark from a local fire set some 70 hectares of scrub forest on fire in the Tarn et Garnonne region.

# Quirks of the culture

## Opening hours

France is a country rooted in tradition, and opening hours in shops are, for the most part, no exception! Most shops stick to 8 / 9am opening, close over lunch time from 12 / 12.30 till 2pm and then reopen until 6 or 7pm. Some large chains or in large cities don't stick to this, but it is still very normal to find the village shop shut over lunch time! For the most part they are also closed on Mondays. This is gradually changing in some areas, but it is worth checking the opening hours if you go out over lunch time or on a Monday so as not to be caught out!

Schools also differ greatly by starting for the most part at 8 and finishing between 4.30 and 5pm. There is no school on a Wednesday afternoon as this is traditionally the afternoon that kids partake in sports.

Many businesses, large and small, still respect the two-hour lunch break.

# Holidays and Observances in France in 2024

| Date | Day | Name | Type |
|---|---|---|---|
| 1st January | Monday | New Year's Day | National holiday |
| 29th March | Friday | Good Friday | Local Holiday |
| 31st March | Sunday | Easter Sunday | Observance |
| 1st April | Monday | Easter Monday | National holiday |
| 1st May | Wednesday | Labour Day / May Day | National holiday |
| 8th May | Wednesday | WWII Victory day | National holiday |
| 9th May | Thursday | Ascension Day | National holiday |
| 19th May | Sunday | Whit Sunday | Observance |
| 20th May | Monday | Whit Monday | National holiday |
| 26th May | Sunday | Mother's Day | Observation |
| 16th June | Sunday | Father's Day | Observation |
| 14th July | Sunday | Bastille Day | National holiday |
| 15th August | Thursday | Assumption of Mary | National holiday |
| 1st November | Friday | All Saints Day | National holiday |
| 11th November | Monday | Armistice day | National holiday |
| 24th December | Tuesday | Christmas eve | Observance |
| 25th December | Wednesday | Christmas Day | National Holiday |
| 26th December | Thursday | St Stephen's day | Local holiday |
| 31st December | Tuesday | New Years Eve | Observation |

It is a common practice in France to take a four-day weekend when a bank holiday falls on a Thursday.

      Holiday in French: *jour férié* (official days off of work), *fête* (religious holidays)

      Holidays in French: *vacances* (vacation)

August is the French holiday month, where it appears that the whole country shuts down! You have to be here to experience it. There is little sense of proportion in what they shut and, for example, restaurants that stand to do well in the holiday season can be found shut. Business seems to grind to a halt, and all is made worse by the main summer bank holiday of 15 th August for the Feast of the Assumption of the Virgin Mary. If you do not book a restaurant very well in advance for a meal on 15th August – and the other of the main holidays - you will not get a table neither for love nor money. Similar issues arise on New Year's Day – an event generally treated with more celebration than Christmas Day. Again, you will find a large number of Restaurants closed. The New Year holiday season often seems to last until the next Monday following.

In the last week of August in 2021 one client went to their favourite cheese shop to buy eggs. There were none available – "because the farm was on holiday".

## Concerts and Festivals

At all times of the year, and particularly in the holiday season, you may chose to go to a concert or similar event and before it starts you have to find your seat. In England and many other European countries if you look from the stage, seat 1, or the lowest numbered seat, is the seat in each row is to the left and the highest numbers are to the right. The French have a totally different system and the auditorium is divided, on an imaginary basis into two halves down the centre. To the left of the dividing line and radiating out wards to the left – looking from the stage - are seats 1,3,5,7,9,11 etc. and from the line radiating out to the right are seats 2.4.6.8.10.12 etc. Do not be surprised then when next door seats are say 11 and 13. The box office has not made a mistake. If the concert is not held in a dedicated arena, it is advisable to take your own fold up chairs as many of the festivities are held in the street or public areas and no sitting spaces are provided.

## Electricity hours

The exact hours and rates will vary from supplier to supplier, but almost all French electricity suppliers offer a normal rate tariff (*heures pleines*) and a cheap rate tariff (*heures creuses*). An example before me is where cheap hours start at 22.32 and finish the next morning at 06.32. In this case, the cheap rate is 25.83% cheaper than the full rate – giving massive savings over the year. For this reason alone, it is very important that units such as a hot water heater are programmed so that they only heat in a cheap period. Also, it is very prudent only to turn on dishwashers, washing machines, and tumble dryers after 22.32!

As of November 2023, a two-part tariff was only available on a very limited basis in the UK and the rates are not fixed but can vary day by day. It is also a comfort to know that household electricity prices in France are some 54% cheaper than in the UK.

## Overhead power lines

If you happen to acquire a house that has overhead high voltage power cables running across your land and if trees are growing underneath that are or might interfere with the cable run, be prepared for the fact that on minimal notice – sometimes 12 hours or less – the electricity supplier may come onto your land and prune the trees that could be a problem. This is quite serious pruning, and they will leave a substantial gap – say 4 meters between the lines and the tree. This happens about every 3-6 years. The supplier has a right to do this, and you cannot refuse. They will leave the cut branches in piles near the trees that have been pruned but they do not take the debris away.

## Buying Non-prescription medication

Unlike many other countries, you can only by non-prescription medications such as paracetamol in a pharmacy. Be careful not to get caught out by para-pharmacies which are often found in the halls of a supermarket and look just like a 'normal' pharmacy, but they only tend to sell "well-being" products such as high-end hair and body products, vitamins, minerals and beauty products along with natural remedies, rather than medication.

## Names and numbers

In France, for all admin purposes, our names are written ALEXANDER Emma and LOCKHART-MIRAMS Andrew. They always use capitals for surnames *nom* and the surname comes first.

The French admin have quite a hang-up about using maiden names and in some cases refuse to use married names. A woman's two Covid 19 vaccination certificates may be in the name SURNAME *née* (born) MAIDEN but her 10-year Carte de Sejour may be in the name MAIDEN *ep.*(married) SURNAME. The health card may also be in the SURNAME. However, the EU Digital Covid Vaccination is in the name MAIDEN and it is close to impossible to get the surname changed to SURNAME. It may also be that her driving license will also be in the name MAIDEN.

The traditional way of addressing a girl or an unmarried woman – *"Mademoiselle"* has almost totally disappeared. Young girls are given no title at all. Older girls, from about 18 upwards, and all women, are most often addressed as *"Madame"*.

A small road may well be shown as *"chemin de \*\*\*\*"*. The identifier of type e.g., *chemin* or *ave* or *bdv* seem often to be always lower case on writing paper but this is not the case on many of the road name plates or on business documents.

House numbers have no apparent rhyme or reason. Someone might be 45 *chemin de* \*\*\* but the next-door house is 117. What this means is that the first gate is 45 meters from the start of the road and the second gate is 117 meters from the start. This explains why an isolated house on a minor country road can be numbered 2890 and the neighbour might be number 3241! On the face of it this can only be the slightest help to La Poste – but they know where the houses are in any case.

It might help others, but you must find the right junction to measure from!

Strikes

The French are known for their love of striking and protests (grève), with the country regularly being brought to a standstill by labour disputes.

One reason is the country's long history of labour activism. French workers have been striking for better conditions and wages for over a century. Another factor is the strength of labour unions in France. French labour unions are some of the strongest and most organized in the world, however, it's not just the culture and history of activism that drives the frequency of strikes in France. The country also has a highly centralized, bureaucratic system of labour relations, which can make it difficult for workers to negotiate with employers. In recent years, there has been a destructive and disruptive element to some of these strikes with, in some cases, violence and property damage. Most strikes are limited to the big cities, with large sections of the city becoming no-go areas, but often public transport can be greatly affected. Strikes are often spontaneous and difficult to predict, but the local news is the best source of information!

## Schools

As already discussed, school times are quite long compared to what you may be used to. There are quite a few other differences to be aware of. Children often start school here as young as 2, as soon as they no longer need nappies!

There is a policy of no religious symbols in national education. Even in catholic schools, children are not permitted to wear a cross for example. In recent years, this rule has somewhat been relaxed, but Gabriel Attal – at that time, Minister of Education, now the prime minister - caused a stir by banning the abaya in schools and has consequently brought to the fore the question of religious secularism in education creating huge debates and discussions.

Private schools do exist in France but not in the same form as in other countries. They are funded to a large extent by the government and are affordable for most people, even on a minimum wage as a bursary *(bourse)* is awarded based on income and the number of children in education within your family.

The traditional packed lunch that many of us grew up with, is not widely practiced in France, with school meals (generally of a surprisingly good quality!) being a very important part of the school day.

Many *collèges* (Age 11 – 15) and *Lycées* (Age 15 – 18) offer boarding facilities during the week, with entry into the establishment on a Monday morning and leaving on a Friday evening. Not very many establishments offer weekend or holiday boarding. In the last year of *collège* children face their first set of exams in the hope of obtaining their *diplôme national du brevet* and in the last year of *Lycée* they take the BAC exams (*Le baccalauréat*).

All the way through the education system, even into university, it is common to maintain a wide range of study subjects. French, maths, history/geography, sciences, sport, and at least one other language are taught alongside any specialist subjects, and children must maintain a good level in all of these to be able to obtain their chosen qualification. Grades are given in the form of a mark out of 20 or by a colour system to give an idea of the level of competency in a subject. To pass the *brevet* or *bac* the child must have an overall average of at least 10. Homework is intense, and as part of the national exams, children are expected to prepare and deliver an oral presentation on a specific subject.

School assemblies - There are none – whereas in the UK there may be one every morning – and possibly chapel as well.

The French president, Emanuel Macron announced on 16th January 2024 a series of measures on education, such as doubling the teaching time of civic education from 5th grade and experimenting with a single uniform. Around a hundred voluntary schools will be involved this year, before the scheme is rolled out across the board in 2026 if the results are conclusive. He also called for more cultural and artistic education, with an emphasis on theatre, and for the reintroduction of graduation ceremonies "this year" at collège. At lycée, universal national service for year two students should be generalised.

# Wednesday afternoons and weekend Sport

There are no school games as we know them in England – school facilities are often very limited, and they often use the local community facilities. All sport is played though local clubs e.g. The United Sports Club Caussade. These are, to a considerable part, funded through local towns with Departmental contribution.

To play any sport as part of a club, you will be required to have a medical certificate and a 'licence' issued by the sport's governing body i.e. for equine activities the licence is issued by the FFE and costs 25 euros for children and 36 euros for adults per year and give you basic insurance cover and often promotional offers such as discounts in certain shops or entry to events. You may well have to pay extra to join a club. A fishing licence is often over 100 euros, and team sports are generally in between the two!

## Dietary requirements

French cuisine. *Coq au vin, boeuf bourguignon, foie gras, quiche Lorraine, steak tartare*…Traditionally, meat is the center piece of all meals here.

Whilst the rest of the world hails France as being the ultimate food destination, vegans and vegetarians are often left wanting as the restaurants do not know what to serve. In a country where eating cheese is almost a religion, meat is seen as an essential element of any meal, and the dairy aisle of your local supermarket goes on forever – being a vegan or vegetarian in France can seem like a challenge.

One of the best ways to avoid a disappointing experience at a French restaurant is to let them know your dietary requirements in advance. It takes a little more planning and organization, but it is worth the extra effort.

While French supermarkets are getting better in terms of the range of vegetarian and vegan products they sell, you probably won't find a whole aisle or section devoted to "free from" products as you would in the UK.

Hospitals have been very slow on the uptake, with very little thought given to the range of meals on offer, but as there has been a 24% uptake in vegetarian or vegan meals over the past few years in France, hopefully this will change! Other dietary requirements such as gluten-free (*sans-gluten*) are becoming better understood. Restaurants will often do their best to accommodate your requirements, and supermarkets are also changing and offering a wider variety of suitable products for dietary requirements.

Disabilities

France has made huge progress in improving accessibility to many public places. The Inter-ministerial Committee for Disability, held in Nancy on 2 December 2016, was an opportunity for the Prime Minister to reiterate the need to rethink and strengthen disability policy in France, in order to make life easier for the people concerned and their careers. Fourteen major initiatives were presented, focusing on the education system, access to employment and housing, accessibility to services and improving social rights and the way in which the specific characteristics of each disability are considered. Three specific measures were identified.

Building a society that is more open to people with disabilities.

Designing responses and care adapted to each person's situation.

Simplifying their daily lives.

In practice this translates to improved accessibility and understanding of individual needs in most shops, government buildings, sidewalks and other public places. Although in some areas, improvements have been slow, it is an ongoing process that is getting better all the time.

# Updates for 2024

*MaPrimeAdapt*

MaPrimeAdapt' provides funding for home adaptation work for the elderly and disabled.

Examples of adaptations funded by MaPrimeAdapt' include replacing a bathtub with a walk-in shower, installing an electric stairlift, fitting handrails, widening doors, adapting floor coverings or providing direct access to the home.

The work is tailored to the specific needs identified in an independent living diagnosis.

## Shopping.

A quick word of warning that most supermarket trollies will often need a coin to be able to use them. This is most often either a 1 euro, 2 euro or 50 cents coin. It is always possible to ask in store, where they will give you a *"jeton"* that you can keep specifically for this purpose.

France is also in the process of moving away from plastic packaging, and shopping bags are included in this. It is possible to buy reusable bags in the supermarket, but it gets expensive if this happens every week, so don't forget to take your previously purchased bags with you each time.

Sales or *soldes* take place twice a year in summer and winter, for a period of four weeks in both cases. These dates are set by the French Commercial Code and apply to the whole of France, apart from certain border departments and overseas departments (Dom) for which the dates may be staggered. You cannot therefore use the word *Soldes* to describe commercial operations outside these official periods.

When I arrived in France, one thing that used to drive me insane was queuing up at the till to be served, and then asked to wait while they answered the phone (which inevitably results in a good 10 to 15-minute wait!). It appears that the phone takes priority over those actually waiting to be served and this is accepted with grace by the locals!

## Seasonal supplies

In the UK you can, for example, buy imported asparagus at almost any time of the year – with it being imported from e.g. China, the top producing country in the world. The French, almost always, only sell seasonal fruit and vegetables whilst they are in season and, again, with asparagus, you will not find it on the market stalls outside the spring. This applies to almost all seasonal fruit, and also to seasonal flowers.

## Restaurant irritations

TV - Unless it is a "Sports Bar" type of restaurant, TV screens, and the accompanying noise, are unusual in the UK. Unless they are at the very top end of the market TV screens are installed in many French restaurants and if there is a national sporting event to be seen the screen and the sound will be on.

## "A Partager"

It is very common and perfectly acceptable to ask, when you order, food, for it to be *"A Partager"* i.e a half portion each for two people. This is particularly useful if pizzas are involved as they can come out in massive portions. In some restaurants, they specifically provide for this on the menu with sharing dishes for 2 or more people. It is often applied to seafood platters and surf and turf type dishes.

## Service Charges

Although there are exceptions, mainly in the major cities and at very upmarket restaurants, almost all restaurant service is *"service compris"* – so your bill is the total of the listed charges, and no tip is needed. Beware however that in some places where there are many restaurants, around a popular city centre square for example, there may be a 10% charge for having the meal served outside. This should be made clear before you sit down but any notification may be hidden, or in minute print on the menu, and the charge comes as a nasty shock at the end of the meal.

## Wood tables and wasps

Whilst undoubtedly a teak/oak/wood table is a very nice adornment in any garden, you will find that they are missing from many French outside seating areas. The simple reason for this is that almost all through the summer the temperatures are high enough to warm the wood to the point where the oils are soft enough for them to sucked by wasps – and also other irritating insects. Even a single wasp can make eating from a table close to impossible. The evidence for this is just a short drive round a few French houses where almost all the outside furniture is plastic!

## Pet owning

A new law aimed at combating animal abuse and strengthening the bond between animals and humans was enacted on 30 November 2021 and includes the introduction of a compulsory "certificate of commitment and knowledge" *certificat d'engagement et de connaissance* for owners of domestic animals including cats, dogs, and horses. Two years after this law was introduced, there is still confusion about who and how this is done. If you own a domestic animal, it is worth asking your vet about this certificate and if you need to apply for one.

Bringing your pet to France.

With the UK's Withdrawal Agreement with the EU now in effect, from 1st January 2021, pet passports are no longer valid for dogs, cats, and other animals registered in Great Britain and Northern Ireland. This means that UK-issued pet passports are no longer valid for travel.

Pets will still be able to travel to France, as well as to other countries in the European Union and Schengen Area, and they won't be subject to lengthy quarantines and strict health regulations as they once did before.

However, the process will require a little more paperwork…

## New Rules for Bringing Your Dog to France After Brexit

If you are planning to bring your dog, cat, or other pets on your French holiday:

Your pet must be microchipped.

Your pet must be vaccinated against rabies.

You must obtain an animal health certificate (AHC) for your pet, within 10 days prior to travel.

Other requirements include a tapeworm treatment for dogs travelling to countries including Ireland and Northern Ireland, but this is not currently required for pets travelling to France.

On arrival, the entrance process remains as it was before. You will be asked to present the above documents and scan your pet's microchip.

## What is an Animal Health Certificate?

Animal health certificates (AHC) can be issued by any vet in the country you are travelling from. They must be issued within 10 days of travelling and are valid for four months from the date of issue. In the UK, you should expect to pay around

£110 for an AHC – fees may vary, so check with your vet.

Each AHC is valid for one trip to the EU, so if you're a second-home owner in France, you will need to do this every time you visit if you want to bring your pets along. The good news is that a single AHC is valid for onward travel in the EU and your return travel to the UK (as long as it's within the stipulated four months).

**Bringing Dogs and Other Pets from France to England**

If you're a Brit living in France after Brexit, you will still be able to bring your pets with you on your UK visits. Pet passports will remain valid for pets registered in the EU for entry into the UK. However, if your pet currently has a pet passport issued in the UK, you will need to change this for a French EU pet passport instead. Your vet should be able to do this for you.

Emails

With very few exceptions, the French seem to be systematically bad at answering emails. They also seem to have an institutional dislike of them. One car garage told a client when he asked for an email address that they had so many emails they never really bothered looking so there was no point in the client writing. You will also find that if you look at the websites for many of the stores, shops or contractors they simply do not have emails listed.

If you are trying to set up a contract do not assume that arrangements set out in emails will be incorporated into contract terms.

Keyboards

Be careful if you think you will buy a computer in France rather than bringing one from England as French keyboards are not in the standard UK or US QWERTY format. Touch typing or even single finger typing is very difficult on a French keyboard.

Cold calling

An alternative to emailing has always been the telephone and most of us use this all the time – particularly given the French aversion to emails – above. Cold calling is, however, a serious problem in France and over half the population report receiving cold calls at least once a week. There are strict rules as to when cold calling is permitted, the number of times contact can be attempted in a month and a prohibition for 60 days if you ask not to be contacted. With certain exceptions, registration with Bloctel - https://www.bloctel.gouv.fr - can block up to 10 numbers but this only relates to marketing calls. Many calls try and avoid marketing by asking you if they can explain, for example, the benefits of double glazing or solar panels. Selling these is not permitted but the canny caller can easily move from advising about benefits into making a sale, or at least a salesman's appointment. Your telephone service provider may also be able to help.

Privacy

French Privacy laws prohibit your taking a photograph or video of someone without their consent. It is not exactly clear what this means. Many take photographs of places and crowds, but someone may object if you are taking what looks like a portrait photo. Where a portrait ends, and a crowd starts is unclear but take care and ask if in doubt.

If you have video surveillance cameras at your home, guests must be informed and any external cameras must not film or feature property that does not belong to you i.e., you can't film your neighbour's driveway or the pavement.

A simple example is that if you have video surveillance cameras at your home, guests must be informed. Any external cameras must not film or feature property that does not belong to you. For example, your neighbour's property, the road or the pavement.

**French Privacy Law and Photography**

Article 10 of the European Convention affirms that there are human rights for the freedom of expression and public rights to receive information. In France this right is not absolute and has to be conciliated with certain individual rights.

Article 9 of the French Civil Code states "Everyone has the right to respect for his private life". This is generally considered to include one's right to their own image, even if it is taken in a public space.

The key consideration, for each photograph, is Consent – see below - i.e. the property owner of the subject, which may be his cottage or his face or whatever, needs to agree to the picture being taken and its publication.

This means that before taking a photo of someone you are required by law to ask the individual's permission. If you want to publish it in any way you have to ask their permission for each specific usage. Any object that is created by or is the copyright of an artist, or designer, must have permission to be published in specific contexts. Any owner of property can assert rights of ownership of property and, again, the photographer needs permission to publish, regardless of whether the image was shot from a public or private space. It is safest to understand "publish" as referring to "making public"

For this reason, and certainly if any form of publication is involved, it is advisable in France to always get a signed written permission by individuals, owners of property and creators of original works, whatever the situation, whether in a public or private space.

**Consent**

This could be divided into three forms:-

Written consent – for each specific usage – and this is in two parts, the taking and the use.

Deemed consent.

No consent.

Written consent.


In France each individual has the exclusive right both to their image and who uses it. Not only publishing the image but even taking the photo of someone, the photographer has to have the individual's permission under French Law.

Further the fact that the person accepts to be photographed doesn't mean that they agree to have their image published.

Permission and consent have to be freely given by the individual and specifically for a certain use. In law it doesn't have to be written but it has to be without doubt – so it is almost impossible to prove permission without a written release. One would even need permissions for use of a school photograph, sporting event etc.

It is recommended that the model release, signed by the individual should also give people information about what their rights are, that they have a choice whether to sign or not and information about the appropriate laws.

See below as to an individual's rights.

**Deemed consent.**

When someone places himself or herself in a public place then there is already a measure of tacit consent presumed, but this is reflected in each individual case. Normally the person only has a right of complaint if he/she is a principal subject in the photo.

If someone is in a photo but not an essential element – or when the person is not recognisable – or is an accessory by chance – say in an image of a public monument, or statue, then it is generally considered that consent is not necessary, the same goes when the person is part of a crowd. But, again, each case is taken on its own merits as to what is considered a crowd, or an accessory or not.

We are all been tempted to take photographs of the local markets and the produce on display. How difficult it is to avoid getting a picture of the stall holder. Some stall holders are happy to be asked if it can be a picture of produce only but you are not likely to be popular asking a busy stall holder who is hard pressed serving a big queue. It may be that the stall holder is not an essential element to a picture of shinny vegetables, but the line is a thin one.

In all circumstances, the person's dignity must be respected. Some personal characteristics are strictly monitored under privacy law and considered very personal and sensitive issues – race, sexual orientation, health, political opinions.

Normally public figures, when going about their public life, such as politicians, sports stars, singers etc. are not required to give their consent in such situations because the right of information supersedes their right to their own image, but this only for journalistic news purposes and not for commercial ones, or for illustration.

Images of public figures must not violate the Privacy law. The images must only deal with the individual's public life and role and not refer to anything which is about the individual's private life, which must not be invaded even though he/she is a public figure.

Note though that an image which was once part of a news event, with a public figure at one time, may be considered less relevant later on and what is then not newsworthy therefore becomes an illustration – and the photographer or publisher can be prosecuted for its publication.

In a convenient summary, it is generally recognised both by case law and legal doctrine that consent is implied or not needed for pictures of

public figures performing their public functions or activities (not in private life),

people shown in a larger group (without distinction of one or more individuals),

people who are present in a public location (unless the depicted person is the main focus of the picture), people related to news events of public interest or public information purposes.

Also in France in a number of legal cases the judges in Courts of law have declared that photographers have the right to take and publish photos of people in public without their knowledge or consent as long as the photos contribute to the public's exchange of ideas or opinions or if they are part of the artistic freedom; for example, a legal case between a street photographer and a non-celebrity woman appearing in a photograph taken without her knowledge and published without her consent in the photographer's book decreed that the photographer's freedom of expression in taking and publishing street photography without the consent of the subject is an important freedom in a democracy: the Judge said that;-

"The right to control one's image must yield when a photograph contributes to the exchange of ideas and opinions, deemed "indispensable" to a democratic society."

Therefore, even though the privacy right in public exists in France, a photograph of a specific identifiable person in a public place can still be taken and published without the subject's consent as long as it can be shown that the photograph contributes to the exchange of ideas or opinions to such a degree that would make the photographer's right to freedom of expression more important to the public interest than the subject's privacy right.

None of this is easy stuff but at least if you know how the law might be applied you can better form your own opinion as to whether to shoot and, if so, how to compose the picture. The balance applies to each photograph and not to all or a group of photographs taken at the same time.

Individual cases – There is a view that one should never take photographs of the Gendarmes. Research suggests there is no absolute prohibition, but the French Government is currently debating possible revisions to Article 9. For safety's sake it would be wise not to take any pictures of either the Gendarmes or the Pompiers et Ambulance service – not least because of the very difficult position we have at present with regard to protests of one sort or another all across France.

**No consent.**

This is probably the most likely event for the photographer, but in every case before you set up the photograph you must have the requirements of consent in mind and make up your own mind as to whether it is safe to proceed.

You could take a beautiful landscape image in France, but, technically, you could not publish it without the consent of the owner of the little cottage in the image. Further, if you had consent at the time the image was taken but the owner then sold on, you would need a new consent from the new owner.

Whilst an owner of a property or object doesn't have exclusive rights over the use of the image of that property or object, they always have the right to oppose the use of the image of that property or object by a third party when the use of the image causes an abnormal problem to them. The wrong here is almost certainly in the publication which would bring the matter to the owner's attention and if there was any apparent commercial link, even if not intended, difficulties could arise.

This refers to images shot from a public space. Taking the picture will not necessarily be by itself against the law, unless someone's private life is affected or private property is invaded, as a result.

Although one hopes that it never happens, there may be occasions when you specifically have to take a photo without consent. This is not a Photograph Group point but if you have a car accident on a road and the other car has cut the corner and is way over the white line and on your side, you will want a photograph of the scene whether or not the driver consents, in the same way you will fill in your own version of the accident form if a joint version cannot be agreed.

**Interpretation**

Everything is seen in its context, for example; the skin colour of someone is not in itself a private item, but if a photo of someone is used to identify or class someone by the colour of their skin then this could go against the privacy law; also if, from an image of someone, one can deduce that person's state of health, this is different to using an image, purposely to show someone's state of health.

So, it is both the context, the use and the purpose of the photographic image which is important; but, again, everything is judged on its individual merits and it depends a lot on the Judge. One Court judgement may be different to another on the same photo. It, of course, always a matter of chance, which Judge is asked to form a view.

French privacy laws confer certain rights to individuals.

Right to be informed about how images will or can be used.

Subject has the right to ask questions, to be informed by what right the person has to take a picture – the photographer has to answer this.

Subject has the right to access information, at any stage they want, and get information by telephone, written communication etc.

A person photographed has the right of opposition, at any time, when they have a serious reason for doing so, for editorial usage.

A person does not need a reason to oppose its use, if the image is used for direct marketing, commerce or publicity.

You could take a picture of a demonstration in Paris. Technically you could be sued if you did not get a consent form signed by everyone recognisable in the photograph. It is unlikely that you would lose the case, but legal representation and a Court case would be required. This is a fair example of the "No consent" option.

Whilst an owner of a property or object doesn't have exclusive rights over the use of the image of that property or object, they always have the right to oppose the use of the image of that property or object by a third party WHEN the use of the image causes an abnormal problem to them.

For photography in all private places, one always needs permission, both of the subject and the owner.

## Peeing

Although you may regularly see a cyclist or driver urinating in public, except in a specifically designated place, it is an offence punishable with a 135 euro fine i.e., by the roadside or anywhere on private land. Being caught may be unlikely but there is a record of a 135 euro fine being imposed on a businessman who stopped in the countryside returning after a lunch meeting, he urinated up against a tree and was seen by the police.

## Government documents

Believe it or not, paper used in public administration, e.g. for tax forms is 8mm longer than standard A4 paper and thus does not fit properly in to filling systems or wallets.

# Observing the culture differences

## Formalities – handshakes, *bises*, and hugs

As we have already said many times, France is steeped in social traditions. We owe the word etiquette to the French. It's no wonder that etiquette and manners play a vital role when socialising in France, *la politesse* reigns supreme in French culture. Misunderstanding the social etiquette in France or not adopting French manners can easily lead to some awkward social situations or send a disrespectful message. It's helpful to learn a little French etiquette before you end up the center of attention.

The appropriate greeting in most circumstances is a handshake. French style handshakes are known to be brisk and light. You should expect a loose grip with only one or two up-and-down movements. If you're not familiar with this light style of handshake, you could easily walk away with the costly wrong impression that the other person is in a hurry to get away from you!

Kissing cheeks across genders is a common greeting among friends and family, but do not attempt to do it until your female counterpart makes the initial move.

*La bise* is more than simply a French tradition; it's a habit, a reflex even. Its origins are mostly forgotten, but this custom has been part of French culture for centuries, and can range from the typical two (common in Paris) up to four kisses in other parts of France. It's not usually a real kiss but rather a brush of the cheek with a kiss sound, or sometimes without any contact or noise at all, typically starting from the left. Hugging is much less common, however, and generally uncomfortable for the French.

## Greetings and 'Good byes'

Everywhere you go it is expected that you greet people you meet, not only socially but very importantly, in shops, cafes, restaurants, garages or indeed wherever. This will be a face-to-face acknowledgement with *"Bonjour"* and if you know them, *"Comment allez vous?"*. They expect the same *"Bonjour"*.

Often if you go into a restaurant, fellow guests who you have never seen before and will never see again, will acknowledge your presence with a *"Bonjour"* and they expect the same reply as you pass by.

If you go into a doctor's waiting room, it is expected that you will acknowledge everyone else waiting and again you will get the same reply.

When leaving a shop, or any other establishment it again is always expected that you will say *"Au revoir"* and / or *"Bonne Journee"* (or with the weekend ahead *"Bon week-end"*).

*"Au revoir"* in Tarn et Garonne is pronounced Of-whaa - but is pronounced with 3 syllables in e.g. Paris (oh-rev-wha)

## Expressions

We love some of the French expressions that are in daily use but have no real translation into English. Examples are: -

*Monsieur Madame* – when you are first greeted. How much nicer than "Chaps", or "Guys", or nothing said at all.

*Bon continuation* – said when your second course is served.

*A tout a l'heure* – see you then / later.

*Bon appetite* – self-explanatory but we have no equivalent other than possibly "Enjoy".

*Voilà* – There it is, there you are but with a wonderful touch of magic. The better version of this is *"Et Voilà"*.

*D 'accord* – yes, that's agreed.

*Merci à vous / je vous remercie* – what a lovely way to say thank you.

*Je vous en prie* – You 're welcome.

*Avec plaisir* – says what it means but it is such a delightful way for a person to acknowledge a thank you.

"Thank you"

Just as saying hello is important, so is saying thank you and goodbye! When leaving a shop, staff will often say "have a good day" or *Bonne journée* and it is expected that you should say "Thank you, you too" – *Merci, bonne journée* or "have a good day, Goodbye" *Bonne journée, au revoir*.

How you say thank you, e.g., for the loan of a piece of equipment from a friend or neighbour varies totally dependent on the Department the lender comes from even if the loan takes place in a different Department. For example, to give a bottle of wine to a friend who has helped would be really offensive if they were brought up in the Averyon but may be very acceptable if they were brought up in, say, Tarn et Garonne.

# Eating times and *aperos*

France, in general, still observes traditional meal rituals. Meals are most often "proper meals" as opposed to snacks like sandwiches and are eaten around the table. There are normally two or three courses at each mealtime. Eating as a family is very, very important. This is mostly observed in the rural areas, and not so adhered to in the large cities. Lunch is between 12 and 2pm and the whole 2 hrs is dedicated to family time and discussion. Family Sunday lunches often with friends, can last until early evening.

The evening meal is usually around 8pm.

The catholic religious festivals such as Christmas and Easter are an excellent example of this with families getting together in large numbers and often spending 5 – 6 hrs at the table with multiple courses.

On the whole, it is seen as rude to interrupt, for example, a tradesman during his lunch break!

Aperitifs are also sacred! Any excuse to get together for drinks and nibbles is a good one! If you are invited to *aperos* or aperitifs, it is seen as good etiquette to take along either a bottle of something or some small nibbles. Be prepared for this ritual to last several hours, especially in the summer or if it is a social occasion!

### Knives and Folks!

Don't be surprised if after your first course at a café or restaurant, when you have finished your first course and carefully placed your knife and folk on the plate for them to clear, your plate is held in front of you, as if they are waiting staff are looking for some type of action from you. They are!!!!! It is common practice for you to keep the same cutlery for both first and second courses. If this happens, just take your cutlery back ready for the second course. It has been experienced, that instead of waiting, the staff just remove your cutlery and place it back besides your glass.

## Music in public places.

As with many countries, there is often background music in shops or public places, much of which is in English, but be aware, the music is not censored, and often the lyrics can be more than colourful!! This also happens with music/advertising on the TV, radio, in public concerts and town/village fetes!

## Integrating into local community.

Large towns and cities are often vibrant with lots of events taking place, but the more rural villages are not left out. Each village has a *comité des fêtes* that organises events in the local area. Summer is the most obvious example, where they often organise night food markets where you turn up and buy food from street vendors – often selling locally produced or homemade food, then take your place at the tables in the village centre and enjoy an evening of good food, company, and music.

The *comité des fêtes* also organise concerts, local hikes or *randonnées*, and various other events. This is a great way to get to know the locals and enjoy the fabulous French hospitality.

Tipping

In parts of France - including cities like Paris, tipping is not expected. It may be that a woman will tip her own hairdresser (as would be the case in the UK) but otherwise tipping is not done or expected.

# Recent developments

## Somewhere to express your customer experience

Non-compliant hotel room, overcharged transport costs, false advertising, counterfeits... To protect foreign visitors while visiting France, especially during such events as the Rugby World Cup and the 2024 Olympic and Paralympic Games, the SignalConso platform is available in English https://signal.conso.gouv.fr/en.

While 14% of the reports on SignalConso concern tourism sectors (travel, leisure, cafes/restaurants), and France is preparing to receive millions of foreign visitors for major sporting events, the platform dedicated to reporting and amicable resolution of consumer problems is expanding its service offering with an English version with a dedicated reporting route for anglophone consumers.

By promoting the amicable settlement of disputes between consumers and professionals, non-French-speaking visitors will find the answer, in English, to any consumer problems encountered during their stay.

For the Directorate-General for Competition, Consumer Affairs and Fraud Prevention (DGCCRF), this version will make it possible to detect fraud specifically targeting tourists more quickly and to identify professionals who are the subject of numerous reports in tourist-oriented sectors.

This English version, also available on SignalConso's mobile app, offers international tourists:

the possibility of identifying a professional in just a few clicks (shops in stores, online shops, leisure, transport, cafes/restaurants, etc.).

the possibility to lodge an alert for any consumer problem: lack of information, hidden service, defective or dangerous product/service, etc.

For any consumer related questions, you may have, you can sign on to

https://www.economie.gouv.fr/dgccrf/2023-rugby-world-cup-and-paris-2024-olympic-and-paralympic-games-consumer-questions

## No more receipts in shops

Automatic receipt printing has come to an end in France since 1st August 2023. This change is being made in the context of the fight against waste and substances dangerous to health. It will nevertheless remain possible to request the printing of the receipt. In the face of this major development for retailers and consumers, new elements have to be taken into account.

The following are concerned:

Receipts produced in sales areas and establishments receiving the public.

Tickets issued by automatic machines.

Bank card tickets.

Vouchers and promotional or discount tickets.

In order to obtain a printed receipt, the consumer will now have to expressly ask the trader. The latter is also required to inform the consumer in a legible and comprehensible manner by means of a display at the place where the payment is made.

**Exceptions**

Some receipts will always be printed automatically after 1st August 2023. The following are concerned:

The receipts for the purchase of so-called 'durable goods', which mention the existence and duration of the legal guarantee of conformity. This applies to household appliances, computer equipment or telephony equipment, for example. The full list of these goods can be found in Article D211-6 of the Consumer Code.

Bank card tickets relating to cancelled or credited transactions.

Tickets issued by machines whose preservation and presentation are necessary to benefit from a product or service.

Cash receipts or other billing documents printed by non-automatic weighing instruments.

Digital Cash receipt solutions

Already available, these solutions replace paper receipts.

These e-tickets will be sent to the buyer:

by SMS.

by e-mail

by message in the buyer's banking application (using the credit card sends the e-ticket automatically to the application).

by QR code (allows you to retrieve your e-ticket from a web page).

# Ecology

### Launch of "My Electric Lease" or *"Mon leasing électrique"* in 2024

The government is introducing a long-term leasing scheme for electric cars at €100 per month. The aim is to enable low-income households to switch to electric cars. To take advantage of the scheme, all you have to do is visit the "My electric leasing" platform and meet the conditions.

### Compulsory sorting of bio-waste – *Tri obligatoire des biodéchets*

You may have read that as from 1 January 2024 households are expected to keep kitchen waste, such as food leftovers, stale bread, and green garden waste separate from other domestic waste, and to dispose of this separately – either in specially provided bins or, excepting fish and meat waste, in a compost heap. This is called biowaste. Local authorities are required to provide designated bins into which biowaste can be put but only a very small percentage have achieved this so far. In theory, there is a 35 euro fine for non-compliance but it has been stated that fines will not be imposed during 2024. This really is a case of what will happen is anybody's guess but be aware of the situation and watch out for a communication from your Local Authority with news of what to do.

## Repair bonus

The amount of the repair bonus for white goods doubles for everyday appliances (washing machines, dishwashers, tumble dryers, hoovers and televisions) in 2024. It is increased for more than twenty products and 24 new items of equipment are eligible. Repair for accidental breakage is now possible.

# Essential driving information

Of course, you can find more detailed information in my Driving and Licensing Pack, but here are some essentials about driving in France.

French law requires that all drivers have the following items in their vehicles at all times, so it's vitally important that you get kitted out before you head off:

Reflective jackets - you'll need one for each occupant, not just the driver.

A warning triangle

Headlamp beam deflectors if necessary

Breathalyser/alcohol test

A GB sticker, or Euro registration plates featuring the GB initials if the car is registered in the UK

Spare bulbs

The French authorities have banned the use of all mobile phones while driving, including those used with a hands-free kit or via a Bluetooth device.

It's just not worth the risk - if you're caught, you could be hit with a €135 fine, so save those calls for when you're not on the road.

## TURN OFF YOUR SPEED CAMERA DETECTORS

Many satellite navigation systems come with speed camera detectors, warning you if you're approaching a camera.

However, this function is illegal in France, so you will need to turn them off. If you don't, then you could be fined a massive €1,500.

Check your satnav manual to work out how to change the settings, or else contact the manufacturer before you leave British shores.

## POLLUTION

If you're planning to drive through Paris, or many other cities in France then you will need to buy a pollution sticker to stick on your windscreen. All cars driving within the restricted areas are required to display a clean air sticker which details how much the car pollutes.

These can be snapped up online for just a couple of pounds and are well worth it - if you don't get one, you could be hit with a fine of up to €135.

## DON'T DRINK

The French may love a glass of wine, but their laws on how much you can drink before getting behind the wheel are much stricter than in the UK.

You are allowed just 0.5mg of alcohol in your blood per 100ml in France - about one small beer - compared to 0.8mg in the UK.

If you have less than three years of experience as a driver, the limit is even lower – just 0.2mg.

## THE SPEED LIMITS

French government have reduced the speed limits on its single carriageways. As a result, the top permitted speed has reduced from 90km/h (around 56mph) to 80km/h (50mph).

**Recent updates for 2024**

Speeding

Drivers are no longer penalised by the loss of licence points for speeding under 5 km/h, but they are still subject to fixed fines ranging from 68 to 135 euros. The reduction of one licence point applies only to speeding between 5 km/h and 20 km/h.

Driving licence at 17

Applicants aged 17 can take the practical test for a category B driving licence and be issued with a driving licence.

☐

# Who to call in an emergency.

| Service | Telephone |
|---|---|
| Medical help/*SAMU* | 15 |
| Police - *Police Nationale - Gendarmerie* | 17 |
| Fire & accident - Sapeurs Pompiers | 18 |
| SOS - all services (recommended when calling from a mobile) | 112 |
| SOS - all services (hearing assisted - via SMS and fax only) | 114 |
| Child in danger(child protection) | 119 |
| Missing Child | 116 000 |
| Out-of-hours doctors (as of January 2017) | 116 117 |
| Emergency: Sea & Lake (calling from land) | 112 or 196 |
| Terror/Kidnapping Hotline | Tel: 197 |
| Poison Treatment | 02 99 59 22 22 |

The caller must:

1. State the location where assistance is needed.
2. State their name and telephone number.

3. State what happened, and if it is still happening.

4. State how many people need help.

5. State if there are weapons involved.

All emergency numbers can be reached from pay phones, without the use of a phone card or money. It is also possible to call emergency numbers from a locked mobile phone (112 might work even when the message "no network available" is displayed).

**European SOS 112**

The number 112 can be dialled to reach emergency services - medical, fire and police - from anywhere in Europe. This Pan-European emergency number 112 can be called from any telephone (landline, pay phone or mobile cellular phone). Calls are free. It can be used for any life-threatening situation, including:

•Serious medical problems (accident, unconscious person, severe injuries, chest pain, seizure)

•Any type of fire (house, car)

•Life-threatening situations (crimes)

# Final word

There are many things in France that might differ from your country of origin, and we hope this book gives you an insight into some of the changes and differences you can expect and that it helps to prepare you for situations that you may not have fully understood before. France is a wonderful place to visit or live, and to really get the most out of your experience, understanding the etiquette, processes and mindset will, We hope, help make your time here far more enjoyable. There are so many wonderful and unexpected places to visit, some amazing local products and cuisine and on the whole, people are friendly and welcoming, especially if you abide by the unspoken rules of society.

Apart from the "Final Word" is a single hint as to how to help yourself if you are struggling with the language or a problem – Smile, in fact smile brilliantly, at the person you are with. There is nothing better than a smile to get past the little difficulties.

One brilliant example of this, and where charm gets you everything, is a sign seen outside a café

*"Un Café – 9 euro"*

*"Un Café – S'il vous plaît – 5 euro"*

*"Bonjour. Un Café – S'il vous plaît – 2.5 euro"*

If you have found this information useful, please remember that for more detailed information on some of these subjects, you can purchase specialised packs from me on the Health system, Driving and Licensing and also for the Home. These packs contain information on all the paperwork and procedures necessary, your responsibilities and rights, what to do in an emergency, along with situation specific translations. They allow you to keep all the relevant information together in one place, and have access to all the contact details you may need. No more searching for the date of your next control technique or looking for the phone number or policy number of your insurance, just fill in all your personal details, add in copies of the relevant paperwork and you are prepared for all eventualities!

Of course, Admin'assist is always here to assist if you need help, information or assistance to achieve your goals and dreams in France. You can find me on

Facebook - facebook.com/emmaalexander82

Website - adminassist82.weebly.com

Instagram Emma Alexander (@adminassist82) •

Or of course give me a ring on (0033) 0676264246 or email alexander.emma@neuf.fr

Here is what some of our clients have to say.

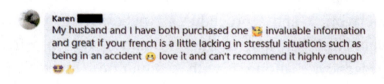

★★★★★ 4 months ago

Emma's knowledge and approach are excellent, and is always available and ready to help no matter what the challenge. We would highly recommend Emma.

Visited in August 2023

We both hope you have a long, happy, and rewarding stay in France.

*Bienvenu en France et vivez votre rêve*

Emma and Andrew

Printed in Great Britain
by Amazon